MW01593408

+ + +
KIDS IN THE
DIVINE SERVICE
+ + +

Presented by way of a cooperation between:

Our Savior Evangelical
Lutheran Church & School
Hartland, Michigan
oursaviorhartland.org

and

The Lutheran Church
Missouri Synod
lcms.org

Cover design, content layout, and
introductory text © 2017, Angels'
Portion Books

Welcome

We welcome you to the house of the Lord! We welcome you to a place and a gathering of people where the Triune God—Father, ✝ Son, and Holy Spirit—makes His presence known among us through the pure preaching of His Gospel and the faithful administration of His holy sacraments.

As our Lutheran Confessions clearly say, the holy Christian church "is the assembly of all believers among whom the Gospel is preached in its purity and the holy sacraments are administered according to the Gospel" (Augsburg Confession, Article VII). Where you find these, you find the Savior, our Lord Jesus Christ. Where you find the Savior, you find "the way, the truth, and the life" (John 14:6), that is, the forgiveness of sins earned for you by Christ through His perfect life, death, resurrection, and ascension. And "where there is the forgiveness of sins, there is also life and salvation" (*Luther's Small Catechism*, The Sacrament of the Altar). In this, we desire whole-heartedly to be present where these wonderful gifts are given. The Psalmist, King David, rejoiced in this eternal truth when he wrote:

> One thing I have desired of the LORD, that will I seek after: that I may dwell in the house of the LORD all the days of my life, to behold the beauty of the LORD, and to inquire in His temple. (Psalm 27:4)

Regarding worship, the Lutheran Confessions also say:

> Thus the service and worship of the Gospel is to receive good things from God, while the worship of the law is to offer and present our goods to God. We cannot offer anything to God unless we have first been reconciled and reborn. The greatest possible comfort comes from this doctrine that the highest worship in the Gospel is the desire to receive forgiveness of sins, grace, and righteousness. About this worship Christ speaks in John 6:40, "This is the will of my Father, that everyone who sees the Son and believes in him should have eternal life." And the Father says (Matt 17:5), "This is my beloved Son, with whom I am well pleased; listen to him" (Apology of the Augsburg Confession, Article IV: 310, Tappert).

The contents of the booklet before you, written by Pastor Christopher Thoma and produced by the Lutheran Church-Missouri Synod, are designed to explain why we do as we do in worship. In the end, and as you'll discover, it isn't us "doing," but God.

Please feel free to read through this booklet before or after worship. If you wish, you may take the booklet home for further study. If you have any questions, don't hesitate to speak with our pastor.

We pray the material provided will serve both you and your family.

Introduction

Children Belong Here

Dearest Visitor,

The Lord spoke clearly, "Let the little children come to me and do not forbid them…" (Mark 10:14). By these words, among other things, Jesus teaches that the company of His flock isn't to be divided. The lambs belong with the rest of the sheep, and as a faithful parent, you are seeing to this.

Now, stick with it!

Do what you can to quietly explain the parts of the worship service, the actions of the pastor, the altar assistants, and the like. If you need help, this pew volume is here at your fingertips and is full of helpful explanations regarding everything your whole family will see and hear.

Remember, too, that children learn the language of faith in the same way they learn to speak their native language—by watching and listening to you! Sing the hymns, fold your hands and pray, participate in the liturgy as best as you can. It will take patience. It will be challenging. But it will be worth it!

Of course, *we don't want to make it difficult for the people around us* to receive what Christ desires for them, and so there is *a certain level of courtesy and common sense* that must be employed for keeping a child in the pews when he or she clearly needs to be taken into a separate space for "parental recalibration" (e.g. screaming at the top of his lungs during the scripture readings, and the like). Nevertheless, don't forget that you and your child belong in the presence of Jesus. Correct and calm your child as best you can and then come back into the service *as soon as you are able!*

Why? Because it's where they belong!

+ + + + +

Dearest Members of this Congregation,

It is one thing to give the above encouragement, but it's another altogether to see it aided by the congregants sharing pews with the little ones. Be aware that the presence of children in this place is not only a gift from God, but it is a visual reminder that He keeps His promise that the gates of hell will never prevail against His Church. Behold, the children!—a simple proof that the Gospel is indeed being preserved for generations to come!

As a seasoned member of this congregation, be sure to greet the little ones with a smile, and do all you can to build up and lovingly encourage their parents, because odds are you've been in their shoes and know the need for such kindly support.

Table of Contents

NAVE and SANCTUARY

LITURGY

GENERAL TOPICS

CHURCH YEAR

KIDS IN THE DIVINE SERVICE

What is Advent?

Advent marks the beginning of the Church Year. Advent is made up of the four Sundays that come right before Christmas. In other words, the deeper into Advent you go, the closer you get to Christmas Day. For Christians, the First Sunday in Advent is kind of like the "New Year's Day" of the Church Year calendar.

Why do we celebrate Advent?

The word Advent means "coming." During Advent, we prepare for the coming of the One who was born that first Christmas in a stable. We prepare for the One who saved us from sin, death and the power of the devil: our Lord Jesus Christ! What a wonderful and exciting time of preparation!

Parents:
At home, in order to help your children better prepare for the birth of Jesus, try using an Advent devotional booklet provided by the church for family devotions.

Copyright © 2016 LCMS Worship. Created by Christopher Thoma. LCMS congregations and schools have permission to reproduce "KIDS in the Divine Service" for their use.
lcms.org | 888-THE LCMS

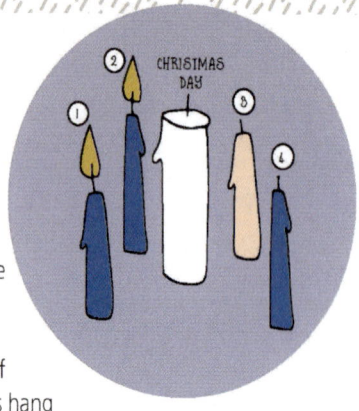

What is the Advent wreath?

The Advent wreath is the circle of candles (and/or evergreen branches) that you see in the sanctuary during the season of Advent. Some Advent wreaths hang from the ceiling of the sanctuary while others are placed on a floor stand. Either way, the Advent wreath is one of the many beautiful things you'll see around the church during Advent.

How do we use the advent wreath?

It used to be that the Advent wreath was used in the home to help count the four weeks of Advent. Now you can find them in homes as well as in the church sanctuary. Each Sunday in Advent, a new candle on the wreath is lit. For example, during the first week in Advent, only one candle is lit. During the second week in Advent, two candles are lit. We do this to remember and prepare for the coming of our Savior, Jesus Christ, the Light of the World!

Parents: Before or after the Divine Service, allow your children to walk up to get a better look at the Advent wreath. Remind them to be reverent in God's holy places. During this Advent season, try utilizing an Advent wreath at home with family devotions. If you are unsure how to get started, ask your pastor for help.

Copyright © 2016 LCMS Worship. Created by Christopher Thoma. LCMS congregations and schools have permission to reproduce "KIDS in the Divine Service" for their use.
lcms.org | 888-THE LCMS

The Advent of Christ

As you may remember, the word Advent means "coming." During the season of Advent, we prepare for the coming of Jesus at Christmas. But that is not the only coming of Jesus that we hear about in the Advent story.

What is the rest of the Advent story?

The Advent of Christ has three parts. God's Word tells us that Jesus not only came to earth as a man at Christmas, but that He comes to be with His church through His Word and Sacraments. Finally, God's Word reminds us that He will return in judgement on the Last Day. If you think about it, there sure are a lot of great things to remember and look forward to during the season of Advent!

Parents:
When Holy Communion is offered, allow your children to attend the altar with you. Remind them that Jesus is truly present here in the Sacrament, and that we will see Him face to face on the Last Day!

 Copyright © 2016 LCMS Worship. Created by Christopher Thoma. LCMS congregations and schools have permission to reproduce "KIDS in the Divine Service" for their use.
lcms.org | 888-THE-LCMS

KIDS IN THE DIVINE SERVICE

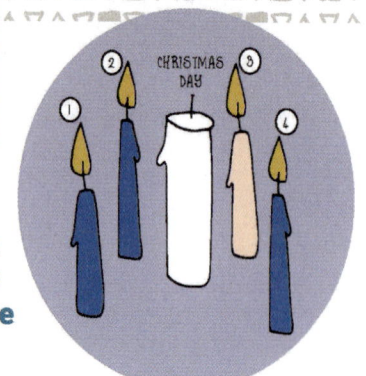

What does it mean when four candles have been lit on the Advent wreath?

You've been preparing and patiently waiting for that wonderful day of celebration. When four of the candles on the Advent wreath have been lit, it means that Christmas is almost here! That's right! The day on which we remember the birth of our Savior is right around the corner!

What does this mean to me?

Today is the Fourth Sunday in Advent. Today is the last Sunday of preparation for the birth of Jesus. Next week the Church will celebrate Christmas Day, one of the most important days of the whole year. As you can see, Advent has prepared us for the coming of Jesus, our wonderful Savior from sin!

Parents:
Remind your children of the important part that Advent plays in the lives of all Christians. This is the time in the Church Year that prepares us for the coming of our Savior. Be sure to bring your children to both Christmas Eve and Christmas Day services.

Copyright © 2016 LCMS Worship. Created by Christopher Thoma. LCMS congregations and schools have permission to reproduce "KIDS in the Divine Service" for their use.
lcms.org | 888-THE LCMS

KIDS IN THE DIVINE SERVICE

The Eve of the Nativity of our Lord

Tonight we begin the season of Christmas. On this night, Christians all over the world are lighting candles, singing hymns and joining together to worship the one true God who made this night so special.

What makes this night different from all other nights?

Tonight is the big night! All through the season of Advent, the Church has been preparing for the birth of Jesus. Tonight we celebrate and remember His arrival! This is the night that our God became a man, born of the Virgin Mary, to save all people from their sins. What a blessed and wonderful night!

Parents: Before or after the service, allow your children to explore the decorations of the church. Instruct them to be reverent in God's holy places. Direct their attention to all of the lights and candles that fill the sanctuary. Remind them that Jesus is the Light of the World. He overcame the darkness of sin and saves all those who believe.

Copyright © 2016 LCMS Worship. Created by Christopher Thoma. LCMS congregations and schools have permission to reproduce "KIDS in the Divine Service" for their use.
lcms.org | 888-THE LCMS

KIDS IN THE DIVINE SERVICE

+ + +
+ + +

What is The Festival of the Nativity of our Lord?

The Festival of the Nativity of our Lord is the traditional way of saying Christmas Day. December 25 is one of the most important festival days in the Church Year. This is the day that we celebrate the birth of our Savior Jesus!

Why do we do the things we do at Christmas?

Many of the things that we do at Christmas have their beginnings with the Romans. Early Christians soon saw some of these things as outward reminders of Christmas and began to use them in their own celebrations. For example, when we give and receive presents, we can remember the greatest gift that has ever been given, our Lord Jesus! After all, today we celebrate Jesus' birthday, and He is the real reason for the season!

Parents: What a great way to spend Christmas! Thanks be to God that you have brought your children to hear the wonderful Good News of Jesus today! When you go home, be sure to remind your children that Jesus is the best present we could ever have. He gave up His life so that we might have eternal life. What a great message to share!

Copyright © 2016 LCMS Worship. Created by Christopher Thoma. LCMS congregations and schools have permission to reproduce "KIDS in the Divine Service" for their use.
lcms.org I 888-THE LCMS

KIDS IN THE DIVINE SERVICE

What is The Festival of the Holy Innocents?

The Festival of the Holy Innocents is the day that we remember the children that were murdered at Bethlehem. These children are considered by some to be the first Christian martyrs. The word martyr (pronouned MAR-ter) comes from a Greek word which means "witness."

What is the whole story of the Holy Innocents?

We learn in Matt. 2:1–18 that King Herod didn't like the idea that a new King was born. He thought that if he killed baby Jesus, his worries would be gone. So he gave orders to have all of the boys in Bethlehem two years and under killed. Herod's soldiers marched into Bethlehem and did just that! But Herod and his soldiers didn't know that an angel had told Joseph in a dream to take Jesus and Mary and escape. When the soldiers stormed Bethlehem, baby Jesus was safe and sound on his way to Egypt. If you think about it, Jesus was saved from death as a baby so that He could die for us a man. What a great and glorious God we have! He keeps His promises!

Parents: Before or after the Divine Service, discuss the meaning of the word martyr. At home, read the story of the Holy Innocents. Be sure to give them examples of other martyrs by reading their stories in Scripture. For example, read the story of Stephen in Acts 6 and 7.

Copyright © 2016 LCMS Worship. Created by Christopher Thoma. LCMS congregations and schools have permission to reproduce "KIDS in the Divine Service" for their use.
lcms.org | 888-THE LCMS

KIDS IN THE DIVINE SERVICE

What is "The Epiphany of Our Lord"?

The word "epiphany" (pronounced ee-PIF-uh-nee) comes from the Greek word meaning "manifestation." Jesus was made known to all people simply by being born. If we had been alive back then, we could have actually reached out and touched Jesus! He was real, and the evidence was in His birth!

Why do we celebrate Epiphany?

Epiphany is the third part of the Christmas season. During this special season in the Church Year, we remember the visit of the Wise Men. Traditionally, this visit is celebrated on Jan. 6.

Epiphany also brings to mind many other important events in Jesus' life. For example, we remember Jesus' Baptism, the star that guided the Wise Men, and most importantly, His birth! Wow! There sure is a lot happening after Christmas!

Parents: "God in flesh made manifest" is a hard statement for children to understand. Be sure to remind them that Jesus is real, alive and once walked on the earth for all to see. When Holy Communion is offered, be sure to let your children attend with you. Instruct them that this is where Christ manifests and gives His true body and blood for us.

 Copyright © 2016 LCMS Worship. Created by Christopher Thoma. LCMS congregations and schools have permission to reproduce "KIDS in the Divine Service" for their use.
lcms.org | 888-THE LCMS

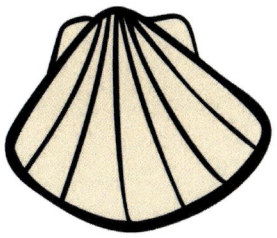

KIDS IN THE DIVINE SERVICE

What is "The Baptism of Our Lord"?

Today is the First Sunday after the Epiphany. Today we celebrate the day that our Lord Jesus was baptized by John the Baptizer. That's right, Jesus was baptized just like you!

Why was Jesus baptized?

Jesus' Baptism is very important. When Jesus was baptized, it marked the beginning of His mission to save the world from sin through His death on the cross and His resurrection from the dead. As Scripture says, Jesus' Baptism was one of the many things He did to "fulfill all righteousness." Because of Jesus and all He has done for us, our Baptism is now a source of forgiveness, life and salvation.

Parents: Before or after the service, allow your children to approach the baptismal font in the sanctuary. Remind them that this is where our life in Jesus begins. Because of God's gifts in Baptism, we have been washed clean, and now we are His children.

Copyright © 2016 LCMS Worship. Created by Christopher Thoma. LCMS congregations and schools have permission to reproduce "KIDS in the Divine Service" for their use.
lcms.org | 888-THE LCMS

KIDS IN THE DIVINE SERVICE

Why was it so important for Jesus to be born as a man?

Jesus had a big job ahead of Him when He was born! If you really think about it, Jesus was born to die on the cross to pay for the sins of the whole world. But before He died, He lived a perfect life under God's Law. That means that during His entire life, Jesus never sinned. Not even once! As a man, Jesus took the place of mankind under the Law and fulilled it. That means that for every time we failed to keep the Law, Christ succeeded!

Why was it important for Jesus to be true God?

It would take more than an ordinary man to suffer and die on the cross to pay for the sins of the whole world. Jesus had to be true God so that He could live a perfect life and fulfill the requirements of the Law, die a perfect death on the cross, and rise from the dead victorious over sin, death and the devil! All of this He did in obedience to the Father and out of complete and total love for us. Through faith, the Holy Spirit delivers all of the great things Jesus won for us in His death and resurrection!

Parents: Review the Ten Commandments with your child (Ex. 20:1–17). Discuss the commandments and be sure to point out just how often we fail to keep them. Remind your child that because of Christ's perfect sacrifice on the cross, in faith we have the forgiveness of sins, life and salvation.

Copyright © 2016 LCMS Worship. Created by Christopher Thoma. LCMS congregations and schools have permission to reproduce "KIDS in the Divine Service" for their use.
lcms.org | 888-THE LCMS

KIDS IN THE DIVINE SERVICE

What is "The Transfiguration of our Lord"?

Have you ever wondered what Jesus might look like in His glory? The Bible gives us a glimpse in the story of Jesus' transfiguration (pronounced trans-fig-yer-A-shun) in Matthew 17. The word "transfigure" means "to change form or appearance." Scripture tells us that Jesus led Peter, James and John up a high mountain. When they got up there, Jesus' appearance changed right before their eyes. His face became as bright as the sun, and His clothes became as white as light.

Why didn't Jesus always appear like this while He was on earth?

If Jesus would have been on earth in His state of glory, He wouldn't have been able to take our place under the Law and then they wouldn't have crucified Him. It was very important for Jesus to die on the cross as a man to pay for our sins. We too will see Jesus as He is in glory on the Last Day! Until then, we see Him: as our crucified and risen Savior revealed to us in the Word and Sacraments!

Parents: Read the story of Jesus' transfiguration in Matt. 17:1–13 with your children. Remind them that we will see Him in glory when we die just as the disciples saw Him on the mountain!

Copyright © 2016 LCMS Worship. Created by Christopher Thoma. LCMS congregations and schools have permission to reproduce "KIDS in the Divine Service" for their use.
lcms.org | 888-THE LCMS

KIDS IN THE DIVINE SERVICE

What is Ash Wednesday all about?

You may see something strange happening in church on Ash Wednesday. You'll see your family and friends go forward to receive the sign of the cross on their foreheads. The strange part about all of this is that it will be done with the ashes from last year's Palm Sunday palm branches.

Why do we do this?

Usually when someone gets dirty they know they need water to get clean. The ashes that are put on our foreheads remind us that in sin we are dirty and need to be cleaned. It also helps us to remember the first time the sign of the cross was made on us at our Baptism. In the waters of Baptism, we are cleaned and the dirt of sin is washed away. Ash Wednesday helps to remind us of this.

Parents: At home after the service, when your children are washing the ashes off, remind them once again that we are washed clean of sin at our Baptism. Jesus did all of this for us through His death on the cross which we prepare for during Lent. Ash Wednesday is the beginning of this time of preparation.

Copyright © 2016 LCMS Worship. Created by Christopher Thoma. LCMS congregations and schools have permission to reproduce "KIDS in the Divine Service" for their use.
lcms.org | 888-THE LCMS

What is "Lent"?

Lent is a season of the Church Year that lasts six weeks. Lent begins on Ash Wednesday and ends the day before Easter Sunday. During these six weeks we look forward to Good Friday, the day our Lord died on the cross to pay for our sins, and to Easter Sunday, the day He rose from the dead to prove it!

How can I remember to think about Jesus during Lent?

You can give up something you enjoy during Lent. You might see your parents give up their morning coffee. Maybe your brother or sister has decided not to eat candy during Lent. Every time you think about doing what you gave up for Lent, it will remind you of what Jesus gave up for you — His life! Blessings to you as you experience the wonderful journey of Lent!

Parents:
We encourage you to help your child decide on something in their life that they can give up during Lent. Be sure to give up something too. Being their example and companion on this journey makes a big difference!

Copyright © 2016 LCMS Worship. Created by Christopher Thoma. LCMS congregations and schools have permission to reproduce "KIDS in the Divine Service" for their use.
lcms.org | 888-THE LCMS

Why do we celebrate Lent for 40 days?

Don't forget what Lent is all about! It is a time when we are reminded of what Jesus gave up for us, and a time when we look forward to and prepare for His death and resurrection!

 We celebrate Lent for six weeks, or 40 days, as we remember Christ's temptation in the wilderness in the Gospel of Matthew. There **Jesus was without food** for 40 days.

 We remember the temptation of **the Israelites in the desert** after the Lord had delivered them from Egypt. This lasted 40 years.

 Finally, we can remember the story of **Noah and his family.** After 40 days and 40 nights of rain, the Lord delivered them as He promised.

During these 40 days of Lent, we remember God's faithfulness to His people and how His faithfulness is complete in Jesus, our Savior. Jesus remains faithful to us, always being where He promises to be: in His Word and Sacraments. Wow! What a Savior!

 **Parents:** Continue to encourage your children in their Lenten preparation. During worship, point out the places where our Lord comes to us (i.e. God's Word, Holy Communion, Holy Baptism, Absolution). Remember, being their example and companion on this Lenten journey makes a difference!

 Copyright © 2016 LCMS Worship. Created by Christopher Thoma. LCMS congregations and schools have permission to reproduce "KIDS in the Divine Service" for their use.
lcms.org | 888-THE LCMS

KIDS IN THE DIVINE SERVICE

Hey! What happened to the "a" word?

There's one word we often use in the Church that isn't used during Lent. Usually we use it after responsories, antiphons and other parts of our worship. Have you guessed what the word is yet? If you guessed "alleluia," then you are right. We stop singing and saying "alleluia" during Lent and won't speak it again until Easter morning.

What does "alleluia" mean and why don't we say it during Lent?

"Alleluia" is a Hebrew word that means "Praise the Lord." Since we focus on the sufferings and death of Jesus during Lent, we stop using this joyful word until we celebrate Jesus' glorious resurrection. On Easter morning the first words you hear will be: "The Lord is risen. He is risen indeed! Alleluia!"

Parents:
During worship, help your children to look for places in the service where "alleluia" has been omitted. Notice the red writing in the hymnal. These words will help to point out when and where we might use or refrain from using the "a" word.

Copyright © 2016 LCMS Worship. Created by Christopher Thoma. LCMS congregations and schools have permission to reproduce "KIDS in the Divine Service" for their use.
lcms.org | 888-THE LCMS

KIDS IN THE DIVINE SERVICE

Why do we have a week called "Holy Week"?

Why would we refer to a week as being holy? The word "holy" means that it is from God. That's why we call the Bible "holy." It isn't just any book. It is God's living Word given to us for our salvation! The same goes for Holy Week. This is "God's Week." This is the week in the Church Year when Jesus actually paid for our sins and won our salvation!

Which days are in Holy Week?

There are particular days during Holy Week that are extra special. During Holy Week we celebrate Palm Sunday, when Jesus went to Jerusalem and people celebrated His arrival; Maundy Thursday, when Jesus instituted the Lord's Supper; Good Friday, when Jesus died on the cross; and Holy Saturday, when we await His resurrection on Easter Sunday!

Parents:
During worship, help your children to look for other things in the church that are considered holy (i.e. God's Word, the Sacraments, etc.). Ask them: "How does God use these things to give us His forgiveness?"

Copyright © 2016 LCMS Worship. Created by Christopher Thoma. LCMS congregations and schools have permission to reproduce "KIDS in the Divine Service" for their use.
lcms.org | 888-THE LCMS

KIDS IN THE DIVINE SERVICE

Why do we celebrate "Palm Sunday"?

The Sunday before Jesus was crucified by the people, they honored and adored Him as their Lord and king with palm branches. We remember this as the beginning of Christ's bitter walk to the cross.

PRAISE HIM!	CRUCIFY HIM!

Why did the people honor and adore Jesus on Palm Sunday and then kill Him on Good Friday?

When Jesus rode into Jerusalem on Palm Sunday, the people began to praise and honor Him as their king. They believed Him to be a powerful leader who would overthrow the Roman government and restore Israel. When Jesus did not do this, the people wanted Him crucified. You and I know what kind of a king He is. He's a king who came to die for the sins of His people. Wow! What a king!

Parents: Remind your children that it was important that Jesus did die for their sins. That is exactly what He came to earth to do. He came to pay the price that we could never pay. Direct your children to the symbols in the church that reflect Christ's death. Remind them that we will hear of His victory over death next Sunday on Easter!!!

Copyright © 2016 LCMS Worship. Created by Christopher Thoma. LCMS congregations and schools have permission to reproduce "KIDS in the Divine Service" for their use.
lcms.org | 888-THE LCMS

If all Jesus had to do was die, then why is Easter such a big deal?

Easter is a very important day. Easter is the day that we celebrate Jesus' resurrection from the dead.

After Jesus was crucified, His disciples were very sad. It seemed like their God and friend had been defeated and killed. They had forgotten that Jesus told them that He would rise from the dead. They must have thought Mary Magdelene was crazy when she told them that Jesus had appeared to her at the tomb where He was buried. But her story was true! Jesus was alive! He had risen from the dead!

Later, Jesus appeared to His disciples many times to prove it. And that's just what He did, *He proved it!* By His resurrection, He proved to the world that He was victorious over death and paid for our sins completely. Now, the first words you hear in church on Easter Sunday are: "The Lord is risen. He is risen indeed! Alleluia!"

Parents: Help your children to recognize the different places in our worship service which speak of Jesus' resurrection (the Creed is a good example). Point out some of the symbols in the church that might aid in their understanding of the resurrection. Remind them that we join in His resurrection through our Baptism!

Copyright © 2016 LCMS Worship. Created by Christopher Thoma. LCMS congregations and schools have permission to reproduce "KIDS in the Divine Service" for their use.
lcms.org | 888-THE LCMS

KIDS IN THE DIVINE SERVICE

What is "Pentecost"?

The word "Pentecost" (pronounced PEN-tuh-kost) comes from the Greek word *pentekostos* which means "fiftieth." Exactly 50 days after Jesus rose from the dead, the Holy Spirit came upon the disciples in the form of flames of fire.

Why is Pentecost so important?

When Jesus died, the disciples were sad because they thought that their friend and Lord was gone forever. But Jesus rose again! Forty days after His resurrection, Jesus did finally ascend into heaven leaving the disciples below. However, before Jesus actually died, rose again and ascended into heaven, He made a promise to His disciples that He would send the Holy Spirit to them. He said that the Holy Spirit would come and guide them "into all the truth" (John 16:13). Jesus doesn't leave us alone to fend for ourselves. Jesus is here with us, and the Holy Spirit guides and leads the Church into the truth of the wonderful Gospel! We celebrate and remember this at Pentecost.

Parents:
At home, read the story of Pentecost in Acts 2 to your children. Remind them that the Holy Spirit comes to us through the Word and Sacraments just as our Lord has promised. Encourage them to thank God for the gift of His Holy Spirit in their lives.

Copyright © 2017 LCMS Worship. Created by Christopher Thoma. LCMS congregations and schools have permission to reproduce "KIDS in the Divine Service" for their use.
lcms.org | 888-THE LCMS

KIDS IN THE DIVINE SERVICE

What is "All Saints' Day"?

All Saints' Day is the day during the Church Year that we celebrate, remember and honor all of those who have died with faith in Jesus and are now with Him in heaven.

Why do we celebrate All Saints' Day?

The word "saint" comes from the Latin word *sanctus* which means "holy" or "sacred." Saints are God's holy people. We thank God for the saints who have gone before us because of their great example of faith and God's great mercy in their lives!

Do you have to die to be a saint?

No way! All of God's faithful people are His saints! We were washed clean of our sins at our Baptism and made holy before God. That's what it means when we hear God's Word say: "These are the ones coming out of the great tribulation. They have washed their robes and made them white in the blood of the Lamb" (Rev. 7:14). Isn't it great to know that it is not what we have done that makes us a saint, but what Jesus has done for us through His death and resurrection? He gives all of this to us through Baptism. He is the one who makes us a saint!

Parents: Talk to your children about those in your own family who have died in the faith. Explain that they are now with Jesus in heaven. Remind them that this is a fulfillment of God's promises at our Baptism.

Copyright © 2017 LCMS Worship. Created by Christopher Thoma. LCMS congregations and schools have permission to reproduce "KIDS in the Divine Service" for their use.
lcms.org I 888-THE LCMS

KIDS IN THE DIVINE SERVICE

What is the "Sunday of the Fulfillment"?

The Sunday of the Fulfillment, which is the last Sunday in the Church Year, is the day we celebrate and look forward to the coming of our Lord Jesus on the Last Day in time.

Why do we celebrate it?

Have you ever had to wait for a really exciting gift that you've always wanted? What was it like when you finally received the gift? The waiting may have been difficult, but when you finally received the gift, it made all of the waiting seem "fulfilled" or complete. As Christians, we are eagerly waiting for our Lord Jesus to return. When he returns, as Scripture says, He will take His people to be with Him in His glorious Kingdom forever. Now that is something to celebrate and be excited about!

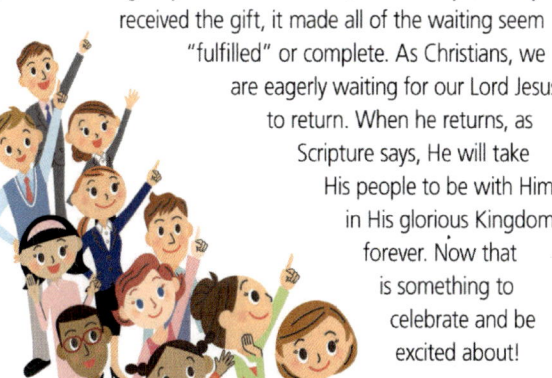

Parents: At home, discuss with your children what will happen when Jesus returns. Take time to read through portions of Matthew 24 and 25. Remind them that in Baptism Jesus makes us His people. Through faith in Him, we live as Christians patiently awaiting His return.

Copyright © 2017 LCMS Worship. Created by Christopher Thoma. LCMS congregations and schools have permission to reproduce "KIDS in the Divine Service" for their use.
lcms.org | 888-THE LCMS

NAVE and SANCTUARY

KIDS IN THE DIVINE SERVICE

What is the "altar"?

When you walk into the sanctuary, what is the first thing you notice? Maybe you see the beautiful stained glass windows. Maybe you noticed the candles. Of all the wonderful sights in our sanctuary, one thing probably comes to your attention first: the altar. The altar is the large, table-like object located directly in the center at the front of the building. The word "altar" comes from the Latin word altare which means "a place for offering sacrifices."

Why do we have an altar when we don't sacrifice anything on it?

It's kind of scary to think that we might use an altar for sacrifice. We look at the altar through the eyes of the Gospel. On the top of the altar are often carved five crosses — one for each of the five wounds of Christ. They mark this altar as a place where no more blood sacrifices will occur. The only sacrifice needed was made on the cross. The altar is a place where Christ gives out the forgiveness He earned for us through His death and resurrection. Wow, the altar sure is an important place!

Parents: During the service, direct your children's attention to the altar. Point out that during the Divine Service this is where God has promised to come to be with us. After the service, take your children up to the altar to observe. Remind them to be reverent in God's holy place.

Copyright © 2017 LCMS Worship. Created by Christopher Thoma. LCMS congregations and schools have permission to reproduce "KIDS in the Divine Service" for their use.
lcms.org | 888-THE LCMS

KIDS IN THE DIVINE SERVICE

What is the "baptismal font"?

In church, the baptismal font is a place where we see the Holy Spirit do His stuff! As St. Paul says in Titus: "He saved us, not because of works done by us in righteousness, but according to his own mercy, by the washing of regeneration and renewal of the Holy Spirit, whom he poured out on us richly through Jesus Christ our Savior, so that being justified by his grace we might become heirs according to the hope of eternal life" (Titus 3:5–7). This all happens at the baptismal font.

Why do we use a baptismal font?

Baptism is important in the lives of God's people. In Baptism you were given the forgiveness of sins, rescued from death and the devil, and given salvation. All of this comes to you through God's Word with the water in Baptism. The font reminds us of the wonderful gift of God's forgiveness. It also reminds us that our old sinful self has been drowned, and a new person arises to live in faith!

Parents: Before or after the service, allow your child to walk up to the baptismal font to get a better look. Remind them to be reverent in God's holy places. During the service, when the sign of the cross is made on the congregation, remind your child that the sign of the cross was made on them at their Baptism. It was there that they were marked as one redeemed by Christ.

Copyright © 2017 LCMS Worship. Created by Christopher Thoma. LCMS congregations and schools have permission to reproduce "KIDS in the Divine Service" for their use.
lcms.org | 888-THE LCMS

Why do we use candles in the Divine Service?

Imagine that you are attending a worship service 500 years ago. Since there are no lights, even during the daytime, the church is dark. How will you see what is going on? How will you see the pastor? How will you walk up to the altar to receive the Lord's Supper? As you probably guessed, one of the first uses for candles in church was to give light in the sanctuary. Actually, oil lamps were probably used until the fourth century when candles became more common.

Is there more to using candles than just lighting the room?

With the invention of the light bulb, candles were no longer needed to light the church. That doesn't mean they lost their importance in the church. Candles have been used for hundreds of years to symbolize Christ's words when he said: "I am the Light of the world" (John 8:12). **Candles remind us that Jesus is the Light that has conquered the darkness of sin.** As you can see, candles play an important role in our worship.

Parents: When the candles are lit at the beginning of the service, remind your children that Christ is the Light of the world. Teach them that when the candles are lit, we are honoring our God and recognizing His presence in the sanctuary. He is really here just as He promised!

Copyright © 2017 LCMS Worship. Created by Christopher Thoma. LCMS congregations and schools have permission to reproduce "KIDS in the Divine Service" for their use.
lcms.org | 888-THE LCMS

KIDS IN THE DIVINE SERVICE

Why is there a rail in the front of the church?

That railing you see up near the altar is the altar rail. Some churches might even have a chancel rail a few steps away from the altar rail nearer to the congregation. **Does your church have both of these rails?**

What are these rails used for?

The chancel rail divides the church into two important parts: the "nave," which is the largest part of the church where the congregation sits; and the "chancel," which is the part of the church where the altar is located. The altar rail separates the altar from the rest of the chancel. It used to be, back in the Middle Ages, these rails were important for separating the congregation from the pastor or priest. As our understanding of the Lord's Supper changed, the rails began to be used for more practical purposes. They became helpful places for God's people to kneel and receive His wonderful gifts. They are also used for confirmation, marriages, and other events in the church.

Parents: Before or after the service, direct your children's attention to the chancel and altar rails. Allow them to walk up to the rails in order to get a better look. Encourage them to make the sign of the cross, kneel and pray. Remind them to be reverent in God's holy place.

Copyright © 2017 LCMS Worship. Created by Christopher Thoma. LCMS congregations and schools have permission to reproduce "KIDS in the Divine Service" for their use.
lcms.org | 888-THE LCMS

KIDS IN THE DIVINE SERVICE

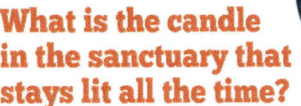

ALL DAY, ALL NIGHT

What is the candle in the sanctuary that stays lit all the time?

I'll bet you can count all of the candles in the church. There are quite a few. If you decide to try, don't forget to count the one that stays lit all the time. That's right, that little light in there is a candle! This particular candle is called an "eternal flame." This candle burns all the time. Look close from where you are sitting. When you find it, maybe you can see it glowing.

Why do we have a candle that stays lit all the time?

When we see the eternal flame we are reminded that God is always present in our lives, and He promises to never leave us. God is especially present in His sanctuary where we hear His living Word and receive his wonderful Sacraments. If the candle burns out, we re-light it or put another one in its place. In other words, we do our best to keep it lit 24 hours-a-day.

Parents: Before or after the service, direct your child's attention to the eternal flame hanging above the altar. Remind them that this candle stays lit all year. Allow them to walk up to the altar in order to get a better look. Remind them to be reverent in God's holy place.

Copyright © 2017 LCMS Worship. Created by Christopher Thoma. LCMS congregations and schools have permission to reproduce "KIDS in the Divine Service" for their use.
lcms.org | 888-THE LCMS

What is the "lectern"?

When the Lord calls us together for worship, He feeds us with His wonderful Word and Sacraments. In most churches, **the Bible sits on a stand called a "lectern."** The word "lectern" comes from the Latin word "lectio," which means "reading."

Why is the Bible read from a lectern?

For thousands of years, God's living Word has been read to His people. When this Word is read to us, we remember that God continues to deliver His promise of salvation to us through faithful preaching and teaching. With the help of the lectern, our church Bible is in a great place for reading to all of God's people!

Parents: Before or after the service, allow your child to walk up to the lectern in order to get a better look. Allow them to look at the church Bible. Remind them to be reverent in God's holy places. During the service, before the readings, remind them that they are about to hear God's Word, and the lectern holds the Bible that they will hear God's wonderful promises from!

Copyright © 2017 LCMS Worship. Created by Christopher Thoma. LCMS congregations and schools have permission to reproduce "KIDS in the Divine Service" for their use.
lcms.org | 888-THE LCMS

What is a "parament"?

A parament (pronounced PAIR-uh-ment) is a colored peice of cloth that hangs on the important items of furniture in the sanctuary. **Can you find the altar?** You may see a colored piece of cloth hanging on it. This parament is called the "frontal" or "superfrontal." **Can you find the pulpit?** The pulpit has a parament, too, as do many of the important furniture items in the sanctuary. Look around to see how many paraments are in your church.

Why do we use paraments?

Paraments honor God and beautify His sanctuary based on the seasons of the Church Year. For example, during the season of Pentecost, the paraments are green. During Lent, the paraments are purple. The word "parament" comes from the Latin word "parare" which means "to decorate or adorn." The paraments are not silent decorations. Each parament helps to proclaim the wonderful news of salvation through Jesus Christ!

Parents: Before or after worship, allow your child to get a closer look at the paraments in the sanctuary. (Remind them to be reverent in God's holy places.) Instruct them that the colors might be different than what they would expect at certain times in the Church Year. For example, the paraments are red on Reformation Day even though it falls during the season of Pentecost.

Copyright © 2017 LCMS Worship. Created by Christopher Thoma. LCMS congregations and schools have permission to reproduce "KIDS in the Divine Service" for their use.
lcms.org | 888-THE LCMS

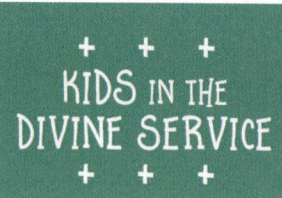

KIDS IN THE DIVINE SERVICE

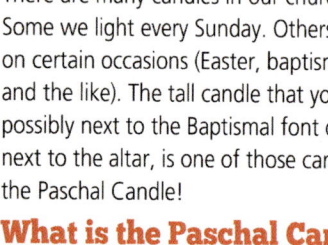

What is that great big candle?

There are many candles in our church sanctuary. Some we light every Sunday. Others we only light on certain occasions (Easter, baptisms, funerals, and the like). The tall candle that you see up front, possibly next to the Baptismal font or up in front next to the altar, is one of those candles. That's the Paschal Candle!

What is the Paschal Candle used for?

The Paschal Candle reminds us of Jesus' victory over death. Do you remember the story of the pillar of fire that led the Israelites at night in the wilderness after the Lord delivered them from slavery in Egypt? When Jesus died on the cross, He released us from the slavery of darkness and death due to our sin. Now, through our Baptism, we have been buried with Him in His death and we are now raised to new life through His resurrection! The Paschal Candle reminds us of this. Let that Gospel light shine!

Parents: Before or after the Divine Service, take your children up to look at the Paschal Candle. Point out the beautiful symbols on its surface that remind us of our Savior and what He has done for us. Remind them that "Jesus Christ is the Light of the world, the Light no darkness can overcome." (*Lutheran Service Book*, 243)

Copyright © 2017 LCMS Worship. Created by Christopher Thoma. LCMS congregations and schools have permission to reproduce "KIDS in the Divine Service" for their use.
lcms.org | 888-THE LCMS

KIDS IN THE DIVINE SERVICE

What is the "processional cross"?

The processional cross is the cross attached to a long pole that is carried into the sanctuary during a processional hymn. During the Entrance Hymn on festival Sundays, a crucifer will carry the processional cross followed by the acolyte and pastor. Maybe you have seen this happen in your church. When the processional cross is not being used in a procession, it sits in a stand in the front of the sanctuary. See if you can find it right now.

Why do we use a processional cross?

When the processional cross enters the sanctuary, we stand to honor our risen Lord and remember that He comes to be with His Church. We especially remember, during festival times in the Church, the reason we are celebrating: Jesus' death on the cross to save us from our sins, and His resurrection to prove it! So, when that cross comes marching in, keep your eye on it. Remember that Christ has come to be with us in His Word and Sacraments. What a wonderful way to begin the Divine Service!

Parents: Before or after the service, allow your child to walk up to the processional cross to get a better look. Remind them to be reverent in God's holy places. During the service, when the cross is being carried in, remind them that our Lord actually comes to be with us every Sunday in His Word and Sacraments. He is really here!

Copyright © 2017 LCMS Worship. Created by Christopher Thoma. LCMS congregations and schools have permission to reproduce "KIDS in the Divine Service" for their use.
lcms.org | 888-THE LCMS

KIDS IN THE DIVINE SERVICE

What is the "pulpit"?

You probably noticed that the pastor preaches to the congregation from the same place in the church almost every time. This place is called the pulpit. The word "pulpit" comes from the Latin word "pulpitum," meaning "scaffold." Do you know what a scaffold is? A scaffold is a platform which is raised high up into the air. If you have ever seen someone washing windows on a building, they were probably standing on a scaffold.

Why do pastors preach from a pulpit?

Before the invention of the microphone, it was sometimes hard to hear what the pastor was saying. By raising the place where the pastor preaches, he could better project his voice for all of the people present to hear the wonderful Gospel. Raising the pulpit above everything else also helps to signify the importance of proclaiming God's pure Word. What a wonderful invention the pulpit is!

Parents: Before or after the service, allow your child to walk up to the pulpit to get a better look. Encourage them to step into the pulpit to get a view of the congregation. Remind them to be reverent in God's holy places. During the service, before the sermon, remind them that pastor is about to preach God's Word and that the pulpit will help them to see and hear him clearly!

Copyright © 2017 LCMS Worship. Created by Christopher Thoma. LCMS congregations and schools have permission to reproduce "KIDS in the Divine Service" for their use.
lcms.org | 888-THE LCMS

KIDS IN THE DIVINE SERVICE

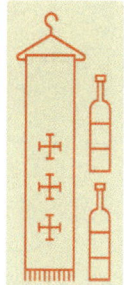

What do we call the room near the sanctuary?

The room near the sanctuary is called the "sacristy." See if you can find the door to the sacristy in your church. The use of sacristies became common over 1500 years ago. In most churches you will find the sacristy beside or behind the the altar area (called the chancel).

What is it used for?

The sacristy is the storage place for the sacred items used in God's house. For example, the vessels and utensils used for Holy Communion are stored there, as well as extra candles, oil and banners. Keeping them in a separate room helps to ensure they are not broken, misplaced or disturbed in any way. Some churches may have two kinds of sacristies. One is the "clergy sacristy" where the pastor keeps his vestments (the clothes he wears during the service). The other is the "altar guild sacristy" where the people who help keep the chancel looking nice store their supplies.

Parents: Before or after the service, allow your children to go into the sacristy to get a better look. Instruct them to be careful. The items there are set aside for use in the service. Help them to remember why the church uses a sacristy.

Copyright © 2017 LCMS Worship. Created by Christopher Thoma. LCMS congregations and schools have permission to reproduce "KIDS in the Divine Service" for their use.
lcms.org | 888-THE LCMS

KIDS IN THE DIVINE SERVICE

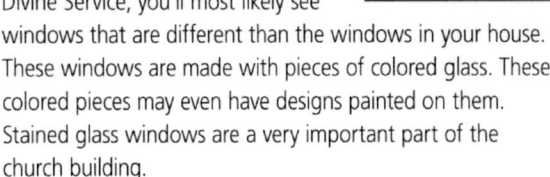

What are the peculiar windows in the church?

If you look around while sitting in the Divine Service, you'll most likely see windows that are different than the windows in your house. These windows are made with pieces of colored glass. These colored pieces may even have designs painted on them. Stained glass windows are a very important part of the church building.

Why do we have stained glass windows in the church?

Stained-glass windows add to the beauty of God's house, but that's not all that they do. These windows are designed to teach us. If you look closely at the windows, you'll find that most of them contain wonderful imagery. This imagery usually depicts stories from the Bible, different Christian symbols or different articles of the Christian faith; and it's all wrapped up in beautiful pictures made from colored and painted glass! What a wonderful way to glorify our Lord and to proclaim the Gospel!

Parents: After worship, be sure to walk around and look at the windows with your child. If there are windows with different themes, take a few moments each week to discuss the individual teaching points of each window. Encourage your child to ask the pastor for help.

Copyright © 2017 LCMS Worship. Created by Christopher Thoma. LCMS congregations and schools have permission to reproduce "KIDS in the Divine Service" for their use.
lcms.org I 888-THE LCMS

LITURGY

What is a "Suffrage"?

A suffrage is a prayer for help. The word "suffrage" comes from the Latin word *suffragium* which means "support." In this type of prayer we ask our Lord to give us His support, assistance and protection. More importantly, we ask Him to keep us strong in the faith and to give faith to other people.

Why is it good to use the Suffrages?

Look at the Suffrages in our hymnal (Responsive Prayer 1, pp. 282–84 in *Lutheran Service Book*). In the morning Suffrages, we ask God to take care of us. In the afternoon or evening suffrages we ask God to protect His Church and world. God commands us to pray in this way (see 1 Tim. 2:1–4). We hear from God's Word that He desires for us to pray for all people. God wants all people to believe in Jesus. In the Suffrages, we pray that God would provide for such salvation. What a wonderful opportunity for us to speak to God on behalf of others!

Parents:
Read through Responsive Prayer 1 with your children. Compare the language in these Suffrages to the language of the Divine Service. How are they similar? How are they different? Be sure to read and discuss 1 Tim. 2:1–4.

Copyright © 2017 LCMS Worship. Created by Christopher Thoma. LCMS congregations and schools have permission to reproduce "KIDS in the Divine Service" for their use.
lcms.org | 888-THE LCMS

KIDS IN THE DIVINE SERVICE

What is the "Offertory"?

The word "offertory" comes from the Latin word *offerre*, which means "to give, or to present." The Offertory is sung by the congregation during the Divine Service as the gifts and offerings are presented to the Lord.

Why do we use the Offertory?

Take a look at the words from the following Offertory: "What shall I render to the Lord for all his benefits to me? ... I will take the cup of salvation and will call upon the name of the Lord." These words from Psalm 116 tell us that the greatest way to praise and thank God for all of His goodness is not the offerings and gifts that we give, but that in faith we continue to receive what He gives us in His Word and Sacraments. Receiving God's gifts isn't just a part of worshiping God, it is the greatest worship of God! Wow! What a wonderful and giving God we have!

 **Parents:** Encourage your children to listen to the words of the Offertory as it is sung. Notice that such words are sung right before the Lord's Supper is prepared and distributed. Here we are receiving the "cup of salvation" full of the Father's grace through the precious blood of His Son, our Lord, Jesus Christ.

 Copyright © 2017 LCMS Worship. Created by Christopher Thoma. LCMS congregations and schools have permission to reproduce "KIDS in the Divine Service" for their use.
lcms.org | 888-THE LCMS

What does the word "Amen" mean?

The word "amen" (pronounced AH-men) is Hebrew for **"certainly"** or **"truly."** Martin Luther said that it really means: **"Yes, yes, it shall be so."** You probably

recognize this word from

hearing it or seeing it used in prayer. Maybe you use it in your prayers every morning when you wake up and every night when you go to sleep.

Why do we use it?

God commands for us to pray. When we use the word "amen" at the end of our prayers, we are letting God know that **we truly believe that He will hear and answer all of our prayers** just as He has promised! What a great way to end a prayer!

Parents: Point out that Jesus used the word "amen" a lot in Scripture when He said things like: "Truly, truly I say to you." Encourage your children to listen for and say "amen" at appropriate points in the service. In what places besides prayer do we hear it amen?

Copyright © 2017 LCMS Worship. Created by Christopher Thoma. LCMS congregations and schools have permission to reproduce "KIDS in the Divine Service" for their use.
lcms.org | 888-THE LCMS

KIDS IN THE DIVINE SERVICE

What does "worship" really mean?

Most people use the word "worship" to mean something we do to honor God. Because of this misunderstanding, many people believe that a church service is what we do for God. The word "worship" comes from the root words "worth" and "ship." These two words describe God rather than the ones praising Him. These words describe a God who is *worthy* of being honored and adored because of His love for us. God gives us His love through His Word and Sacraments. Worship is not something we do, but rather something that God does for us!

What makes the Divine Service so important?

The Divine Service is not about what we are doing for God, but who God is and what He does for us in the ways He has promised: His Word and Sacraments. That's why Lutherans call it *Divine Service*. God is serving us! What a wonderful God we have!

Parents: The Divine Service is like listening to one long reading from the Bible. Everything in the Divine Service has been given to us through God's Word. Explain this to your children, reminding them that it is God's Word that delivers God's salvation to us!

Copyright © 2017 LCMS Worship. Created by Christopher Thoma. LCMS congregations and schools have permission to reproduce "KIDS in the Divine Service" for their use.
lcms.org | 888-THE-LCMS

KIDS IN THE DIVINE SERVICE

What is a "canticle"?

The word "canticle" (pronounced KAN-ti-kle) comes from the Latin word "cantus," which means "song." A canticle is a song based on a text from Holy Scripture. What could be better than to sing praises to God with the words He gives us?

What's the difference between a canticle and a hymn?

Hymns and canticles both put God's Word to music. You'll know you are singing a hymn when all of the verses are sung to the same melody. You'll know you are singing a canticle when the verses continue without repeating the melody. What glorious variety our Lord gives in the Divine Service!

Parents: The best way to differentiate between canticles and hymns is to look and listen. Usually the "songs" in a hymnal are appropriately designated as a hymn or a canticle. Help your children to compare the differences. You can see and hear the differences. Point out the differences and discuss the words. Take a look at the texts in the Bible that have inspired the canticle or hymn.

Copyright © 2017 LCMS Worship. Created by Christopher Thoma. LCMS congregations and schools have permission to reproduce "KIDS in the Divine Service" for their use.
lcms.org | 888-THE LCMS

What is a "hymn"?

The word "hymn" comes from a Greek word which means "song of praise." Webster's Dictionary tells us that a hymn is "a song of praise especially in honor of God." In the Church, we sing hymns because they are God's Word put to music. What an awesome way to praise our Lord!

Why do we sing hymns?

During the early years of the Christian Church, its music came from the Psalms. As new people came into the Church, they added new hymns. The Church's hymns have stood the test of time, never failing God's people as generations change. When we sing hymns, we are praising God with the words He has already put on our tongues! There is no better way to pray, praise, and give thanks to God than with the words He has given us.

Parents: In order to answer questions as to why we do what we do as Lutherans, including utilizing the hymnody, read the introduction on pages 6 and 7 in *Lutheran Worship*. Here you will find a brief summary of what Lutheran worship and hymnody are all about.

 Copyright © 2017 LCMS Worship. Created by Christopher Thoma. LCMS congregations and schools have permission to reproduce "KIDS in the Divine Service" for their use.
lcms.org | 888-THE LCMS

What is a "psalm"?

If you open a Bible to the middle, you might find the book of Psalms. The psalms are prayers and praises to God. During Old Testament times, the psalms were sung during worship in the temple. The book of Psalms was like the hymnal of the Old Testament.

Why do we sing them in church on Sunday?

Many of the psalms were written for use in worship. Christians have been singing psalms to the Lord since the beginning. Colossians 3:16 instructs us to use pslams, "Let the word of Christ dwell in you richly, teaching and admonishing one another in all wisdom, singing psalms and hymns and spiritual songs, with thankfulness in your hearts to God."

 **Parents:** Before or after the service, show your child where to find the book of Psalms in the Bible. Remind them that these are prayers and praises to God that He gave to us. There's no better way to worship than with the words He has given! Try using one in your devotions at home.

 Copyright © 2017 LCMS Worship. Created by Christopher Thoma. LCMS congregations and schools have permission to reproduce "KIDS in the Divine Service" for their use.
lcms.org | 888-THE LCMS

KIDS IN THE DIVINE SERVICE

What is the "Agnus Dei"?

The "Agnus Dei" (pronounced AHN-yus DAY-ee) has been sung by the Church for almost 1,200 years. "Agnus Dei" is Latin for "Lamb of God." We usually sing these words in the Divine Service after the Words of Institution have been spoken by the pastor.

Why do we use the Agnus Dei?

In John 1:29, John the Baptizer proclaims, through the power of the Holy Spirit, that Jesus is the "Lamb of God, who takes away the sin of the world." He said this as Jesus was walking up to him. When we sing the Agnus Dei, like John the Baptizer, we are once again hearing, proclaiming and learning the great Gospel message which confesses that Christ is here with us in Holy Communion, giving us His very body and blood for the forgiveness of our sins. What a great way to recognize the real presence of Christ in the Sacrament!

Parents:
After the Divine Service, read John 1:29–34 with your children. Compare John the Baptizer's words to the Passover story in Ex. 12:1–11, 21–23. Be sure to discuss why John calls Jesus the "Lamb of God." Jesus was the ultimate sacrificial Lamb of God by whose death we have been rescued from sin, death and the power of the devil.

 Copyright © 2017 LCMS Worship. Created by Christopher Thoma. LCMS congregations and schools have permission to reproduce "KIDS in the Divine Service" for their use.
lcms.org | 888-THE LCMS

KIDS IN THE DIVINE SERVICE

What is "making the sign of the cross"?

Making the sign of the cross means to draw an invisible cross on yourself at certain times during personal prayer, the Divine Service and other appropriate times during worship.

How do I make the sign of the cross?

Hold your thumb and two fingers together. ① Touch your forehead, ② then your tummy, ③ your left shoulder, ④ then your right shoulder ⑤ and finally your chest. Try it a few times and you'll get it. Before long, it will be easy to do!

Why is it a great thing to do?

Can you think of a time when your pastor first made the sign of the cross on you? At your Baptism, you received the sign of the cross on your forehead and on your heart to mark you as one redeemed by Christ! Making the sign of the cross is a great way to remember all that Jesus has done for you on the cross and given to you in and through Baptism!

Parents: Before or after the service, practice making the sign of the cross with your children. Remind them that we may make the sign of the cross at certain times during the service, for example, anytime you see a small red "cross" symbol, or pastor makes the sign of the cross on the congregation.

Copyright © 2017 LCMS Worship. Created by Christopher Thoma. LCMS congregations and schools have permission to reproduce "KIDS in the Divine Service" for their use.
lcms.org | 888-THE LCMS

KIDS IN THE DIVINE SERVICE

What is "Matins"?

Today we receive our Lord's gracious gifts through the Order of Matins. The word "Matins" comes from the Latin word "matutinus" which means "of the morning." Matins is a service of prayer that is used by the Church **in the morning.**

Why do we use the Order of Matins?

The Order of Matins has been used by Christians since almost the beginning of Christianity. At the beginning of the day, Christians prayed the Order of Matins because it started their day off right! You can use the Order of Matins too! When you wake up in the morning, grab your hymnal and try it. What better way than to begin each morning deep in God's wonderful Word? If you're not sure how to do it, then ask your pastor. He'd be glad to help you!

Parents: It can be quite easy for children to learn and enjoy the liturgy of the Church when a parent shows them how. Children rely upon routines in their lives, which are put in place by parents. Matins can become a part of the morning devotional routine at your house.

Copyright © 2017 LCMS Worship. Created by Christopher Thoma. LCMS congregations and schools have permission to reproduce "KIDS in the Divine Service" for their use.
lcms.org | 888-THE LCMS

KIDS IN THE DIVINE SERVICE

What is "prayer"?

Have you ever wanted to talk to God? Well, guess what … you can! God promises to hear and answer us when we pray. Because we want to concentrate on what we are praying and who we are praying to, we may close our eyes, fold our hands and bow our heads so that we are not distracted by the things around us. You don't have to do all that, though. You can pray anywhere and at anytime.

What should we pray for?

We not only ask God for what we need, but we praise and thank Him for what He has already given us. If you want to, you can pray to God just to talk to him. We pray especially that God would keep us strong in our faith, and that He might bring others to faith too.

Are there different types of prayer?

There are many different types of prayer. Much of our worship is prayers, including the Confession, the Agnus Dei, and the Post-Communion Canticle. You can find prayers for different times and needs on pages 305–18 in *Lutheran Service Book*.

Parents: Direct your child to the different prayers in our worship. (For example The Prayer of the Church) Turn to pages 327 in *Lutheran Service Book*. Read through Luther's Morning and Evening Prayers. Try using them at home with your children when they wake up in the morning and before they go to bed at night.

Copyright © 2017 LCMS Worship. Created by Christopher Thoma. LCMS congregations and schools have permission to reproduce "KIDS in the Divine Service" for their use.
lcms.org | 888-THE LCMS

KIDS IN THE DIVINE SERVICE

What is the "Benediction"?

The Benediction (pronounced ben-eh-DIK-shun) is God's blessing for the congregation given through the pastor at the very end of the service. There are several different benedictions that we use in the church. The Aaronic Benediction is the one that we use in the Divine Service. You can find this in Num. 6:24–26. We use the other benedictions in other services like Matins and Vespers. Can you find the benedictions for these services in your hymnal?

Why is there a Benediction in the Divine Service?

The word "benediction" comes from the Latin word *bene* which means "well," and *dicere* which means "speak." When the pastor pronounces the Benediction, God is giving us His blessing, or speaking well to us. He sends us on our way with His blessing after we have received His wonderful gifts through the Word and Sacraments. God sure does a lot of giving to His people!

Parents:
Before or after the Divine Service, direct your children to the various services in the hymnal. Encourage them to find and read the benedictions for each service. Help them to find the Aaronic Benediction.

 Copyright © 2017 LCMS Worship. Created by Christopher Thoma. LCMS congregations and schools have permission to reproduce "KIDS in the Divine Service" for their use.
lcms.org | 888-THE LCMS

What is the "Collect"?

The word "collect" (pronounced COLL-ect) comes from the Latin word *collectus* which means "gathered together." A Collect is a prayer to God which **gathers together** the thoughts of the congregation into one prayer for the day.

Why do we use a Collect in the Divine Service?

We use the Collect in the Divine Service because it focuses the congregation's prayers and attention on the readings from God's Word, which will be read shortly after the Collect. The Collect highlights the theme of the Sunday throughout the Church Year.

Parents: Before the Collect is prayed in the service, remind your children to pray in their minds along with the pastor. Encourage them to pay close attention to his words. Encourage them to listen for the theme in the collect and in the Gospel reading.

Copyright © 2017 LCMS Worship. Created by Christopher Thoma. LCMS congregations and schools have permission to reproduce "KIDS in the Divine Service" for their use.
lcms.org | 888-THE LCMS

KIDS IN THE DIVINE SERVICE

What is the "Gradual"?

The Gradual is the responsive reading that takes place between the Old Testament Reading and the Epistle Reading. The Gradual can be a Psalm or another portion of Scripture appropriate for the day.

Why do we do this in the Divine Service?

The word "Gradual" comes from the Latin word *gradus* which means "step." As you can probably guess from its name, the Gradual is a stepping stone from one reading to another. In other words, after we read from God's Word in the Old Testament, we use God's Word in the Gradual to step to God's Word in the Epistle. Wow! There sure is a lot of God's wonderful Word in the Divine Service!

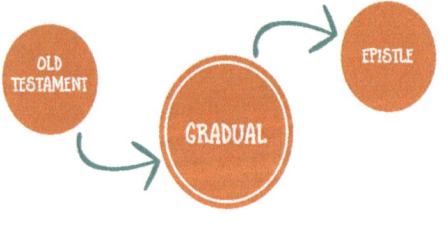

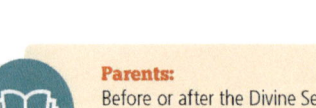

Parents:
Before or after the Divine Service, direct your children to the Gradual for the day. Remind them to concentrate on God's Word throughout the Divine Service.

Copyright © 2017 LCMS Worship. Created by Christopher Thoma. LCMS congregations and schools have permission to reproduce "KIDS in the Divine Service" for their use.
lcms.org | 888-THE LCMS

KIDS IN THE DIVINE SERVICE

What is the "Introit"?

The Introit (pronounced in-TRO-it) comes from the Latin word *introitus* which means "entrance." The Introit used to be sung as the Pastors came into the church and approached the altar.

Why do we use the Introit in the Divine Service?

Usually, the Introit is a Psalm, or parts of Psalms, put together to help sketch a picture of the theme for the day. Sometimes the Introit can be portions of other books of the Bible. For an example of this, the Introit for "All Saints' Day." comes from a Psalm and the book of Revelation, but all of it comes from God's Word!

Parents:
Before or after the Divine Service, look through the service for the Introit. Be sure to point out the one theme that ties all the parts of the service together: our Savior, Jesus Christ.

Copyright © 2017 LCMS Worship. Created by Christopher Thoma. LCMS congregations and schools have permission to reproduce "KIDS in the Divine Service" for their use.
lcms.org I 888-THE LCMS

What is the "Offering"?

This is the time during the service when we offer gifts to God with the rest of the congregation. The Offering is concluded with the *Offertory*, which is the song that we sing while these gifts are being presented at the altar.

Why do we give some of our money to the Church?

The money that we give goes to help support all the work of the church. If you think about it, all that we have is a gift from God. When we give an offering, we are saying thanks to God for all of His wonderful gifts. As Christians, we give to God in response to what He has given to us: life; food; family; and, most important, our Savior Jesus! We don't give because we have to, we give because, in faith, we want to!

Parents: Before the Divine Service, remind your children what giving to the Offering means. Help them to think of all the things that they have and how they are really gifts from God. Encourage them to set aside a certain amount of their own money each week to give.

Copyright © 2017 LCMS Worship. Created by Christopher Thoma. LCMS congregations and schools have permission to reproduce "KIDS in the Divine Service" for their use.
icms.org | 888-THE LCMS

What is the "Offertory"?

The word "offertory" comes from the Latin word *offerre*, which means "to give, or to present." The Offertory is sung by the congregation during the Divine Service as the gifts and offerings are presented to the Lord.

Why do we use the Offertory?

Take a look at the words from the following Offertory: **"What shall I render to the Lord for all his benefits to me?** ... I will take the cup of salvation and will call upon the name of the Lord." These words from Psalm 116 tell us that the greatest way to praise and thank God for all of His goodness is not the offerings and gifts that we give, but that in faith we continue to receive what He gives us in His Word and Sacraments. Receiving God's gifts isn't just a part of worshiping God, it is the greatest worship of God! Wow! What a wonderful and giving God we have!

Parents: Encourage your children to listen to the words of the Offertory as it is sung. Notice that such words are sung right before the Lord's Supper is prepared and distributed. Here we are receiving the "cup of salvation" full of the Father's grace through the precious blood of His Son, our Lord, Jesus Christ.

Copyright © 2017 LCMS Worship. Created by Christopher Thoma. LCMS congregations and schools have permission to reproduce "KIDS in the Divine Service" for their use.
lcms.org | 888-THE LCMS

KIDS IN THE DIVINE SERVICE

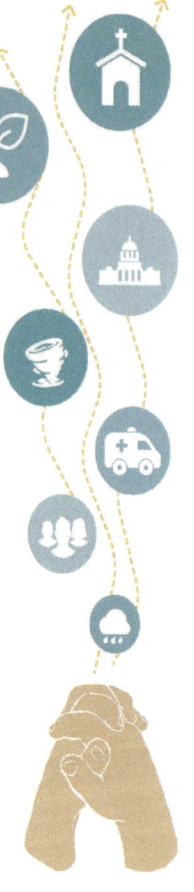

What is the "Prayer of the Church"?

The Prayer of the Church (or the "Prayers") is the time of the service when the pastor leads the congregation in a series of petitions, or prayers. Each prayer is introduced by a "bid," an invitation to the congregation to join in each of these prayers. The bid is not part of the prayer, but it gathers the congregation's thoughts together and directs them toward the specific petitions and thanksgivings that we are about to pray.

Why is this so important?

Do you know anyone who needs God's care? During the Prayers, we pray for all the people of our congregation, particularly those who are sick and shut-in. We also pray for our government, for all believers and many others. No wonder it is called the Prayer of the Church!

Parents:
Before the Divine Service, remind your children to pay close attention to the words of the prayers. Encourage them to concentrate along with the rest of the congregation. Try using bids in your family prayers.

Copyright © 2017 LCMS Worship. Created by Christopher Thoma. LCMS congregations and schools have permission to reproduce "KIDS in the Divine Service" for their use.
lcms.org | 888-THE LCMS

KIDS IN THE DIVINE SERVICE

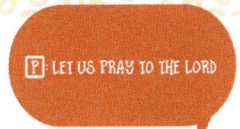

P- LET US PRAY TO THE LORD

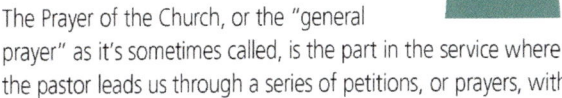

What is the "Prayer of the Church"?

The Prayer of the Church, or the "general prayer" as it's sometimes called, is the part in the service where the pastor leads us through a series of petitions, or prayers, with

R- LORD, HAVE MERCY

responses from the congregation. For example, after each petition the pastor may say: **"Let us pray to the Lord,"** and the congregation may respond with **"Lord, have mercy."** See if you can find the Prayer of the Church in your hymnal. Try to find the other response that the pastor and congregation might say.

Why do we do this in the Divine Service?

Do you know anyone who needs praying for? Wouldn't you like to have the rest of the congregation praying for that person too? During the Prayer of the Church, we pray for all of the people of our congregation, particularly those who are sick and shut-in. We also pray for our missionaries, for our government, for all believers and many others. No wonder it's called the Prayer of the Church!

Parents: Before the Divine Service, remind your children to pay close attention to the words of the prayers. Encourage them to join in the responses with the rest of the congregation. Try using these responses in your prayers at home.

Copyright © 2017 LCMS Worship. Created by Christopher Thoma. LCMS congregations and schools have permission to reproduce "KIDS in the Divine Service" for their use.
lcms.org | 888-THE LCMS

KIDS IN THE DIVINE SERVICE

What is the "Sanctus"?

The Sanctus (pronounced sahnk-TOOS) is a hymn of praise sung during the order of Holy Communion. The word *sanctus* is the Latin word for "holy." The Sanctus begins "Holy, holy, holy! Lord God of power and might: Heaven and earth are full of your glory." We sing the same words sung by the angels in Isaiah 6, about the glory of our God who has come to be with us. Then we sing "Hosanna in the highest. Blessed is he who comes in the name of the Lord. Hosanna in the highest." These words from Psalm 118 were sung by the crowds when Christ rode into Jerusalem on Palm Sunday.

Why do we sing the Sanctus?

The Sanctus proclaims that our Savior Jesus comes to be with us physically in His very body and blood for the forgiveness of our sins. He is really and truly present in the Sacrament of Holy Communion! When we sing the Sanctus, the angels in heaven along with those who have died in the faith join us in a hymn of praise to God. Wow! That is amazing!

Parents: The Sanctus proclaims the presence of Christ in the Sacrament while praising God and confessing the unity of God's Church in every time and place. Encourage your children to sing the Sanctus with the congregation. Remind them that Jesus is really here and that they are singing the Sanctus with people and spiritual beings they can't even see!

Copyright © 2017 LCMS Worship. Created by Christopher Thoma. LCMS congregations and schools have permission to reproduce "KIDS in the Divine Service" for their use.
lcms.org | 888-THE LCMS

KIDS IN THE DIVINE SERVICE

What's a "Kyrie"?

The Kyrie comes from the Greek words "kyrie eleison" (pronounced KEER-ee-ay eh-LAY-zon) which means **"Lord, have mercy."** You've probably noticed that we sing this after we have confessed our sins and received God's forgiveness. For example, look to see where the Kyrie is in the Divine Service.

Why do we ask the Lord to have mercy on us after we have already confessed our sins and been forgiven?

When we sing the Kyrie, we are not making a confession of sins. Instead, we are crying for mercy so that our God would hear us and come to help us in all times of need. It is the first prayer that we pray together in the Divine Service as God's forgiven people!

Parents:
During worship, help your children to recognize the Kyrie and its place in our worship. You may want to practice saying "Kyrie Eleison" with them. After thay have mastered the pronunciation, praise them for having learned a bit of the Greek language!

Copyright © 2017 LCMS Worship. Created by Christopher Thoma. LCMS congregations and schools have permission to reproduce "KIDS in the Divine Service" for their use.
lcms.org | 888-THE LCMS

KIDS IN THE DIVINE SERVICE

Why is Confession so important to a Christian?

Confessing our sins is important! When we confess them, we see just how terribly sinful we are.

We also know that sin brings nothing but eternal death and separation from God. When we confess our sins, not only do we see that we are sinful, but we admit to God that we deserve death and separation from Him forever. We are free to admit all of this to Him because we know that Jesus has already died and paid for all of our sins.

After we have confessed our sins, is there any hope?

After Confession comes Absolution, or, the forgiveness of sins! In Jesus we have the sure and true promise of forgiveness of sins. "If we confess our sins, he is faithful and just to forgive us our sins and to cleanse us from all unrighteousness" (1 John 1:9). Wow! Absolution is *absolutely* wonderful!

Parents: Before the service, read through the confession and explain the words that might be confusing. During the service, help direct your children to the Confession/ Absolution as it happens. Remind them that when the Pastor is speaking, it is as if God himself is speaking these words of comfort to us.

Copyright © 2017 LCMS Worship. Created by Christopher Thoma. LCMS congregations and schools have permission to reproduce "KIDS in the Divine Service" for their use.
lcms.org | 888-THE LCMS

KIDS IN THE DIVINE SERVICE

Every Sunday morning, God's people gather together to receive the wonderful gifts of salvation. The gifts that our Lord has for us are delivered in different ways. One of these very important ways is the sermon.

Why is the sermon so important?

Some people don't like the sermon. They think it is too long, or maybe it is too boring. Some people even try to think of other things while the pastor is preaching. When we are tempted to think this way, we must remember what the sermon is all about. In the sermon, **the wonderful Gospel message of Christ** and all that He has done for us on the cross is proclaimed. Through the sermon, the pastor brings this great message to people right where they are. Though we see and hear our pastor in the puplit, The words of the Gospel are spoken to us and all people by Jesus, saving all from their sins. Wow! What a great way to actually hear the voice of our Savior!

Parents: Before church, remind your children that Jesus speaks to them directly during the sermon. Let them know that the message is not just for adults, but for Jesus' little lambs too! Encourage them to sit and listen to Jesus as he tells them the Good News. If they get lost in the sermon, comfort them by, after the service, explaining things that might have been confusing.

Copyright © 2017 LCMS Worship. Created by Christopher Thoma. LCMS congregations and schools have permission to reproduce "KIDS in the Divine Service" for their use.
lcms.org I 888-THE LCMS

77

GENERAL TOPICS

KIDS IN THE DIVINE SERVICE

What is an "acolyte"?

The acolyte is the person (or persons) who lights the candles before the service. The word acolyte comes from the Greek word *akolouthos* which means "follower." In English, the word acolyte sometimes means "attendant."

Why do we use acolytes in the Church?

Acolytes have always been an important part of worship. For centuries, acolytes have attended to the service of God's people by helping the pastor in many different ways. In our

churches today, acolytes primarily serve by lighting the candles. Acolytes wear robes and sit apart from the congregation because they are helping the pastor to serve God's people during the service. Wow! What an important job!

Parents:
During the Divine Service, point out the acolyte to your children. If they are too young at the time, encourage them that one day they will get the opportunity to be an acolyte. Remind them that being an acolyte is a very important job for children to have in the church.

Copyright © 2017 LCMS Worship. Created by Christopher Thoma. LCMS congregations and schools have permission to reproduce "KIDS in the Divine Service" for their use.
lcms.org | 888-THE LCMS

A great big word of love.

A word that you often hear used in the church is the word "redemption" (pronounced ree-DEMP-shun). All of the events in Jesus' life work together to form God's plan of redemption.

What does "redemption" mean?

The word "redemption" is a very important word used to describe what Jesus has done for us. Redemption comes from the root word "redeem" which means "to buy back." God's plan of redemption was His plan to buy us back from sin, death and the power of the devil. This all happened when Jesus fulfilled the requirements of the Law perfectly and died on the cross in our place. He payed the high price for sin, and He bought us back! But He didn't stop there. He overcame death for us and rose from the dead to prove it! What a great Redeemer we have!

Parents:
What our God has done for us in Jesus reflects the Fatherly love He has for all people. As parents, we share this love with our children through the means our Lord has provided: Word and Sacrament. This is where we receive the real fruits of redemption.

Copyright © 2017 LCMS Worship. Created by Christopher Thoma. LCMS congregations and schools have permission to reproduce "KIDS in the Divine Service" for their use.
lcms.org | 888-THE-LCMS

Another great big word of love

In the Bible we hear the wonderful Good News of Jesus and all He has done for us. We hear about how He has saved us from our sins through His perfect life, death and resurrection. What you may not know is how the Holy Spirit fits into the picture. "Sanctification" (pronounced sank-ti-fi-KAY-shun) is the word used by the Church to describe this.

What does "sanctification" mean?

"Sanctification" comes from the root word "sanctify" which means "to make holy." The Holy Spirit sanctifies, or makes us holy, by giving us faith in Jesus and enabling us to do good works. All of this He does for us through the wonderful Gospel, and the Gospel can be found all wrapped up in the Word and Sacraments. Wow! The Holy Spirit is really at work in our lives!

Parents: Our Savior paid the price, and the Holy Spirit delivers the gifts! What a great combination and promise. Before or after the service, visit the baptismal font with your children and remind them that this is where the work of sanctification began. In Baptism we are washed clean and made holy before God!

Copyright © 2017 LCMS Worship. Created by Christopher Thoma. LCMS congregations and schools have permission to reproduce "KIDS in the Divine Service" for their use.
lcms.org | 888-THE LCMS

KIDS IN THE DIVINE SERVICE

What is a "catechism"?

A catechism (pronounced KAT-eh-kizm) is a book of instruction usually written in question and answer form. The word "catechism" comes from the Greek word *katekhein*, which means "to instruct." A catechism teaches the basics of the Christian faith.

Why do we need catechisms?

While visiting local churches, Martin Luther found many pastors and their church members were unaware of the true teachings of the Bible. Because of this, the people were living immoral lives. Martin Luther wrote the catechisms to instruct people in the basics of the Christian faith, that they might know Christ and His forgiveness and live accordingly. We still use Luther's Large and Small Catechisms so that we never forget those things that are necessary for faith in Christ.

Parents: Consider these words from Luther: "I, too, am a theologian who has attained a fairly good practical knowledge and experience of Holy Scriptures through various dangers. But I do not so glory in this gift as not to join my children daily in prayerfully reciting the Catechism. ... For God gave the Word that we should impress it on ourselves. ... Without this practice our souls become rusty, as it were, and we lose ourselves" (Plass, Ewald M., *What Luther Says* vol. 1 [St. Louis: Concordia, 1986], 125–26).

Copyright © 2017 LCMS Worship. Created by Christopher Thoma. LCMS congregations and schools have permission to reproduce "KIDS in the Divine Service" for their use.
lcms.org | 888-THE LCMS

KIDS IN THE DIVINE SERVICE

What are "ceremonies"?

The word "ceremony" comes from the Latin word that means "ritual." Ceremonies are the actions associated with the words we use in worship. For example, when the Pastor says "In the name of the Father, and of the Son, and of the Holy Spirit" you may see people making the sign of the cross. Making the sign of the cross is a ceremony. Can you think of other ceremonies that occur during the Divine Service?

Why do we have ceremonies?

Ceremonies help to keep things reverent and in good order during worship, but **their main purpose is to teach the faith through sight, sound and action.** For example, when we make the sign of the cross, we are reminded of our Baptism. At your Baptism, you received the sign of the cross on your forehead and on your heart to mark you as one redeemed by Christ the crucified! Ceremonies also show what a congregation believes. You can learn a lot about a church by the ceremonies in their worship.

Parents: The Lutheran Confessions say: "The purpose of observing ceremonies is that men may learn the Scriptures," and "the chief purpose of all ceremonies is to teach the people what they need to know about Christ." If you have questions about the ceremonies of your church, ask your pastor. He will be happy to explain them!

Copyright © 2017 LCMS Worship. Created by Christopher Thoma. LCMS congregations and schools have permission to reproduce "KIDS in the Divine Service" for their use.
lcms.org I 888-THE LCMS

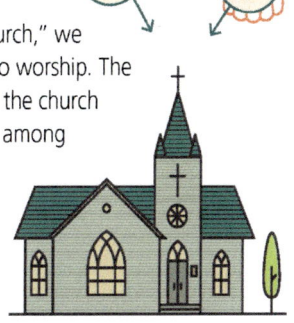

What is the "church"?

When someone says the word "church," we usually think of a place people go to worship. The Lutheran Confessions teach us that the church is the "assembly of all the believers among whom the Gospel is preached in its purity and the Holy Sacraments are administered according to the Gospel." Wow! The church is so much more than a building!

If the church is more than just the building, then why is the building and everything in it so important?

The church building, or the "sanctuary," is a place where God is present. We know that our Lord has promised to come to us in His Sacraments. Since God is actually here with us in His house, we should be very reverent, or respectful. We don't want anything in the church pulling us away from what God gives us in His Word and Sacraments. Everything should direct our attention toward Him.

Parents: Before or after the service, direct your children to the wonderfully Gospel-rich symbolism found in the sanctuary, including the on the altar, windows and banners. Remind them that the Lord truly comes to us here in His Word and Sacraments. He brings us what we really need: the forgiveness of sins.

Copyright © 2017 LCMS Worship. Created by Christopher Thoma. LCMS congregations and schools have permission to reproduce "KIDS in the Divine Service" for their use.
lcms.org | 888-THE LCMS

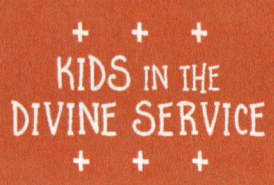

What is a "Gospel Procession"?

You may sometimes see the Gospel reading take place in a different part of the church. On special Sundays, the Bible is carried into the center of the congregation where the pastor reads the Gospel to the people. There may also be some festive music or singing. After the reading, while the Bible is being carried back to its place, there may be more music and singing. This ceremony is called the Gospel Procession.

Why do we have a Gospel Procession?

Jesus is the living Word. He set us free from the burden of sin through His life, death and resurrection. A Gospel Procession reminds us that this wonderful news is to be carried into the whole world. Jesus came for all people and He offers eternal life to all who believe by the power of the Holy Spirit! Wow! A Gospel Procession is a wonderful thing!

 **Parents:** Before or after the Divine Service, remind your children of the meaning of the Gospel Procession. When it is taking place, point out the reverent way the pastor, crucifer, and/or assistants move. Reverence and humility are shown to the One who is truly among us declaring the Good News of forgiveness of sins by His Word! Read John 1:1–3, 14 and discuss it with your children. How is Jesus described in this reading?

 Copyright © 2017 LCMS Worship. Created by Christopher Thoma. LCMS congregations and schools have permission to reproduce "KIDS in the Divine Service" for their use.
lcms.org | 888-THE LCMS

KIDS IN THE DIVINE SERVICE

Who is the Holy Spirit?

The explanation of the Small Catechism says, the Holy Spirit is "the third person in the Holy Trinity, true God with the Father and Son." This means that we believe in one true God, in three persons: the Father, the Son and the Holy Spirit. The Holy Spirit is God just as the Father is God and the Son is God.

What does the Holy Spirit do?

The Holy Spirit sanctifies God's people. In other words, He makes us holy by giving us saving faith in Jesus and the strength to lead godly lives in His name.

Why is the Holy Spirit so important?

We need the Holy Spirit and what He gives to us, because without Him, we are not able to believe in Jesus. In 1 Cor. 2:14 we hear the following: "The natural person does not accept the things of the Spirit of God, for they are folly to him, and he is not able to understand them because they are spiritually discerned." The Holy Spirit calls us to faith through the Gospel and delivers the gracious gifts of salvation in the Sacraments.

Parents:
During the service, tell your children to listen for times the Pastor says the name of the Holy Spirit (i.e. the Invocation, Benediction). Remind your children that the Holy Spirit is exactly where God promised us He would be — in the Word and Sacraments. He comes to us by no other means than through these gracious gifts.

Copyright © 2017 LCMS Worship. Created by Christopher Thoma. LCMS congregations and schools have permission to reproduce "KIDS in the Divine Service" for their use.
lcms.org | 888-THE LCMS

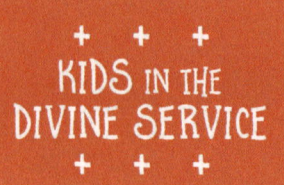
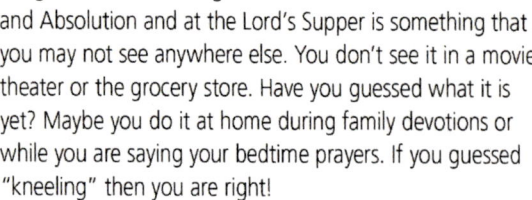

What are people doing on their knees?

During the Divine Service we do things that may seem a little weird. One of the things that we do during Confession and Absolution and at the Lord's Supper is something that you may not see anywhere else. You don't see it in a movie theater or the grocery store. Have you guessed what it is yet? Maybe you do it at home during family devotions or while you are saying your bedtime prayers. If you guessed "kneeling" then you are right!

Why do we kneel in the Divine Service?

Kneeling is a good way to show true humility in the Divine Service, because God is truly present. The King of Kings, Jesus Christ, comes to be with us. It is here that He gives us the good gifts of forgiveness, life and salvation. Paul says, "Therefore God has highly exalted him and bestowed on him the name that is above every name, so that at the name of Jesus every knee should bow, in heaven and on earth and under the earth, and every tongue confess that Jesus Christ is Lord, to the glory of God the Father" (Phil. 2:9–11).

Parents: Encourage your children to watch for different times during the Divine Service when the congregation kneels. Practice kneeling during family devotions and during personal prayer time. Be a living example of this gesture of humility.

Copyright © 2017 LCMS Worship. Created by Christopher Thoma. LCMS congregations and schools have permission to reproduce "KIDS in the Divine Service" for their use.
lcms.org | 888-THE LCMS

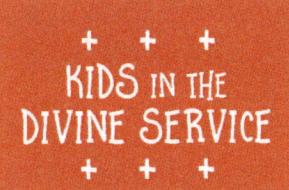

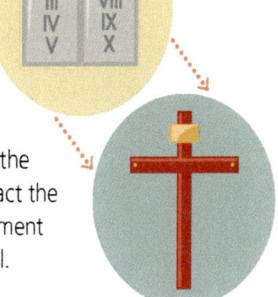

Law and Gospel

Many people wrongly think that the Old Testament is the Law and the New Testament is the Gospel. In fact the Old Testament and the New Testament each contain both Law and Gospel.

What are the basics of the Law and the Gospel?

The Law teaches us God's will for how we live, namely the Ten Commandments. God's Law demands perfection, but it is impossible to be perfect. According to the Law, we are sinners, and are in big trouble with God. We need someone to save us. The Law shows us our sins.

The Gospel tells us what Jesus has done to save us from our sins. But the Gospel doesn't stop there. It tells us what Jesus continues to do for us because of His great love for us. The Gospel shows us our Savior, Jesus!

An easy way to remember all of this is to think of the following letters: S.O.S. The Law "shows our sins" while the Gospel "shows our Savior"!

Parents: Distinguishing between Law and Gospel is a life-long venture of study. Perhaps you or your child can take notes during the sermon. Following the Divine Service, discuss these notes, identifying the Law and the Gospel in the sermon.

Copyright © 2017 LCMS Worship. Created by Christopher Thoma. LCMS congregations and schools have permission to reproduce "KIDS in the Divine Service" for their use.
lcms.org | 888-THE LCMS

KIDS IN THE DIVINE SERVICE

What is the date today?

Usually when someone asks this question, you might look to a calendar for the answer. The date might help determine what to wear, where to go, and what you might do. For example, if the date were January 15, you might decide to wear warm winter clothes. If it were July 12, your family might have a picnic. Calendars help keep things in order.

What does this have to do with the Divine Service?

The Church's calendar determines much of what happens in worship each Sunday (like the colors in the Sanctuary, or the readings for the day). The Church has its own calendar and its own seasons. The Church's seasons are based on the different events in the life of Christ and His Church. Instead of Summer, Fall, Winter and Spring, the Church's calendar has Advent, Christmas, Lent and many more. This calendar helps put order to the seasons and festivals of the Church.

Parents: Before or after the service, direct your children to the front of the hymnal to find the liturgical calendar. Go through the calendar and discuss the different seasons. Remind them that many of the special dates we have on our everyday calendars come from the liturgical calendar, i.e. Christmas, Easter, etc.

Copyright © 2017 LCMS Worship. Created by Christopher Thoma. LCMS congregations and schools have permission to reproduce "KIDS in the Divine Service" for their use.
lcms.org I 888-THE LCMS

KIDS IN THE DIVINE SERVICE

What is the "Office of the Keys"?

When you hear this question, you might think that there is an office somewhere in the church building that holds a lot of keys. But this use of "office" means duty and obligation. For example, when someone is elected to Congress, they are elected to a public office with authority and certain duties. The Office of the Keys is an authority given by Christ to His Church with the duty to forgive repentant sinners, but to withhold forgiveness from the unrepentant as long as they do not repent.

Why is this authority called "keys"?

This authority given to the Church works just like a set of keys that locks and unlocks the gates of heaven. When forgiveness is withheld, the door of heaven is locked. When forgiveness is given, the door of heaven is opened and God's forgiveness in Christ is poured out on the repentant person!

Parents: Trying to understand why the Church would withhold forgiveness may be difficult. Be sure to study John 20:22–23 and Matt. 18:18 with your child. Discuss what it means to be unrepentant as opposed to repentant. An unrepentant person is not sorry for their sins and does not believe in Jesus Christ. A repentant person is sorry for their sins out of love for God and believes in Jesus Christ for salvation!

Copyright © 2017 LCMS Worship. Created by Christopher Thoma. LCMS congregations and schools have permission to reproduce "KIDS in the Divine Service" for their use.
lcms.org | 888-THE LCMS

KIDS IN THE DIVINE SERVICE

What are "rites"?

No, "rites" are not the opposite of "wrongs," though it might sound that way. In the church, rites are the words and texts of the Divine Services and Prayer Offices. **Almost all of the rites in our hymnal are straight from the Bible.**

Why do we use rites?

Rites make up a majority of our worship services. These rites are the written words of our God as they have been given to us in the Bible. In these rites we hear the voice of our Savior, Jesus, proclaiming with His own words His victory over sin, death and the power of the devil. He is giving to us the forgiveness of sins which He won for us when He died on the cross and rose again at Easter. There is nothing better than for Christ's church to worship using such wonderful rites!

Parents: Before or after the Divine Service, discuss the meaning of "rites" with your child. At home, choose portions of the Divine Service and study the purpose of the rites used. Encourage your children to recognize the importance of a worship life grounded in God's Word and Sacraments, which the rites of our hymnal provide. Be sure to ask your pastor if you have any questions.

 Copyright © 2017 LCMS Worship. Created by Christopher Thoma. LCMS congregations and schools have permission to reproduce "KIDS in the Divine Service" for their use.
lcms.org | 888-THE LCMS

KIDS IN THE DIVINE SERVICE

What are "rubrics"?

A rubric (pronounced ROO-brik) is a direction for conducting a service. The word "rubric" comes from the Latin word rubrica which means "red chalk." Can you guess which words in our hymnal are the rubrics? If you guessed those words written in red, then you are right! They are red to make them look different from the words of the service.

Why do we use rubrics?

We all need directions so that we know what to do. **Rubrics offer direction to the pastor and the congregation during the service.** For example, the rubrics may tell us which page to turn to next. The rubrics may even tell us when to stand and when to sit. Rubrics help to keep everything in good order during the Divine Service. What wonderful tools the rubrics are!

Parents:
Take a few moments before or after worship to look at the different rubrics in the hymnal, then choose a few to discuss. Why are they so important? How might the directions which they give be helpful to us? How do they prepare us for the Divine Service?

Copyright © 2017 LCMS Worship. Created by Christopher Thoma. LCMS congregations and schools have permission to reproduce "KIDS in the Divine Service" for their use.
lcms.org | 888-THE LCMS

KIDS IN THE DIVINE SERVICE

What is a "steward"?

A steward is someone who has been put in charge of something. For example, if you are a babysitter, you are a steward for the parents of the child you are watching. We have been entrusted as stewards, or keepers, of God's creation. That means that He has given us everything we have, and out of love for Him, we use all things for His will. This includes giving of our time, talents, money and all that we have in service to Him.

Why do Christians give?

Like everyone else, we belong to God because He created us and sustains us. As Christians we belong to His kingdom of salvation through our Baptism. God's love motivates us to give of what we have. We don't give because we owe God for all He has done for us in Jesus. Instead, we give because of the powerful Gospel that is working within us! Wow! God really strengthens us for wonderful service!

Parents: Before or after the service, discuss stewardship with your children. Remind them why we give. Help them to discover how they might give of what they have. Encourage them to set aside a certain portion of their own money each week to give. They will experience the joy of giving first-hand.

Copyright © 2017 LCMS Worship. Created by Christopher Thoma. LCMS congregations and schools have permission to reproduce "KIDS in the Divine Service" for their use.
lcms.org | 888-THE LCMS

Do Lutherans honor and remember the saints?

Yes. Remembering and honoring the saints is very "Lutheran." God's Word and the Lutheran Confessions teach that remembering and honoring the saints is a great thing to do.

Why is it such a great thing to do?

The Apology of the Augsburg Confession, which explains what Lutherans believe, teaches that we honor the saints for three reasons. (1)Thanksgiving. When we honor the saints, we thank God for "showing (his people) examples of his mercy, revealing his will to save men, and giving teachers and other gifts to the church." (2)Strengthening our faith. When we see how our Lord forgives the saints, we are "encouraged to believe that grace does abound more than sin."(Do you remember when Peter, one of the disciples, denied Jesus three times? Even the Apostles sinned and received forgiveness.) (3)"the imitation, first of their faith and then of their other virtues …" We pray that God would keep us as strong in the faith as they were!

Parents: Explain to your children that we are not praying to the saints; we are simply honoring them on a special day in the Church Year. Remind them that, when we die, we will be with our Lord in heaven, which is where the saints are right now!

Copyright © 2017 LCMS Worship. Created by Christopher Thoma. LCMS congregations and schools have permission to reproduce "KIDS in the Divine Service" for their use.
lcms.org | 888-THE-LCMS

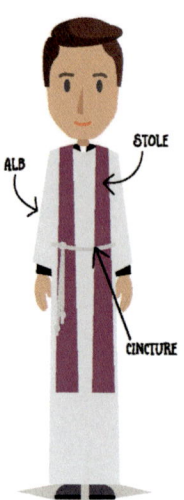

ALB **STOLE**

CINCTURE

What are "vestments"?

When you first see the pastor and his assistants in the Divine Service, what do you notice about them? They are wearing long robes and other unique garments. These are called "vestments." The word "vestment" comes from the Latin word *vestimentum* which means "garment of office." Vestments are garments worn by the pastor and the assistants during the Divine Service and other prayer offices.

Why are vestments used?

A person's vestment tells us about who they are and their role during the Divine Service. If you have two or more pastors, one may be dressed in vestments that mark him as the presiding minister. The other pastors may be dressed in vestments that mark them as assisting ministers. Vestments help to keep the proclamation of the Gospel and administration of the Sacraments in good order. Did you know that God's people have been using vestments since Old Testament times? Wow! Vestments are great tools in the church!

Parents: Before the Divine Service, direct your child's attention to the pastor's vestments. What color are they? How are they different from what you are wearing? Be sure to let your child approach the pastor after church to ask him questions about the vestments.

Copyright © 2017 LCMS Worship. Created by Christopher Thoma. LCMS congregations and schools have permission to reproduce "KIDS in the Divine Service" for their use.
lcms.org | 888-THE LCMS

KIDS IN THE DIVINE SERVICE

Why do we worship on Sunday?

Do you remember on what day Jesus rose from the dead? On what day did Jesus appear to His disciples on the road to Emmaus? If you guessed Sunday, you are right! The Early Church gathered on Sunday because it directed our attention to Jesus' resurrection from the dead. Many other miraculous events in the early Christian Church, such as Pentecost, happened on Sunday.

When did Christians begin gathering together for worship on Sundays?

We know from the Bible that during Paul's lifetime Christians met on Sunday to hear God's Word and celebrate Holy Communion (Acts 20:7; 1 Cor. 16:2). Though Christians in different regions of the world sometimes worshipped on different days, by A.D. 325 most Christians worshipped on Sunday because they considered it "the Lord's Day." Wow, what a great tradition we share with our Christian ancestors!

Parents: In the Early Church, Christians used different terms for their day of worship such as "First Day" or "Eighth Day." The label "the Lord's Day" stands out as the most significant title chosen by the Church. Direct your children to the significance in having a particular day set aside for receiving God's wonderful gifts through Word and Sacrament.

 Copyright © 2017 LCMS Worship. Created by Christopher Thoma. LCMS congregations and schools have permission to reproduce "KIDS in the Divine Service" for their use.
lcms.org | 888-THE LCMS

Angels' Portion Books

Made in the USA
Middletown, DE
25 February 2020

85077760R00055